Christopher Columbus

Recognizing Stereotypes

Titles in the opposing viewpoints juniors series:

Advertising	Garbage	The U.S. Constitution
AIDS	Gun Control	The War on Drugs
Alcohol	The Homeless	Working Mothers
Animal Rights	Immigration	Zoos
Causes of Crime	Nuclear Power	
Child Abuse	The Palestinian Conflict	
Christopher Columbus	Patriotism	
Death Penalty	Pollution	
Drugs and Sports	Population	
Elections	Poverty	
Endangered Species	Prisons	
The Environment	Smoking	
Forests	Television	
Free Speech	Toxic Wastes	

Christopher Columbus

Recognizing Stereotypes

Curriculum Consultant: JoAnne Buggey, Ph.D.
College of Education, University of Minnesota

By Bonnie Szumski

Greenhaven Press, Inc.
Post Office Box 289009
San Diego, CA 92198-9009

Cover photo by: The Granger Collection

Library of Congress Cataloging-in-Publication Data

Szumski, Bonnie, 1958-
　　Christopher Columbus : recognizing stereotypes / by Bonnie Szumski ;
　curriculum consultant, JoAnne Buggey.
　　　p. cm. — (Opposing viewpoints juniors)
　Includes bibliographical references and index.
　　Summary: Presents different viewpoints on the importance of
Columbus in the discovery of America. Includes critical thinking
activities to help the reader recognize stereotypes.
　ISBN 0-89908-069-3
　　1. Columbus, Christopher—Juvenile literature. 2. America—
Discovery and exploration—Spanish—Juvenile literature.
[1. Columbus, Christopher. 2. America—Discovery and exploration—
Spanish. 3. Critical thinking.] I. Buggey, Joanne. II. Title. III. Series.
E111.S98　1992
970.01'5—dc20　　　　　　　　　　　　　　　　　　　92-19873
　　　　　　　　　　　　　　　　　　　　　　　　　　　CIP

No part of this book may be reproduced or used in any other form or
by any other means, electrical, mechanical, or otherwise, including, but
not limited to, photocopy, recording, or any information storage and
retrieval system, without prior written permission from the publisher.

Copyright 1992 by Greenhaven Press, Inc.

CONTENTS

The Purpose of This Book: An Introduction to Opposing Viewpoints 6
Skill Introduction: Recognizing Stereotypes 7
Sample Viewpoint A: Christopher Columbus was a hero 8
Sample Viewpoint B: Christopher Columbus was a creep 9
Analyzing the
Sample Viewpoints: Identifying Stereotypes 10

Chapter 1

Preface: Did Christopher Columbus Discover the New World? 11
Viewpoint 1: Christopher Columbus should be credited with
discovering the New World 12
Viewpoint 2: Christopher Columbus did not discover the New World 14
Critical Thinking Skill 1: Recognizing Stereotypes 16

Chapter 2

Preface: Is Christopher Columbus's Legacy in the New World Positive? 17
Viewpoint 3: Christopher Columbus's legacy is negative 18
Viewpoint 4: Christopher Columbus's legacy is positive 22
Critical Thinking Skill 2: Recognizing Stereotypes in Statements 26

Chapter 3

Preface: Should Columbus's Voyages Be Celebrated? 27
Viewpoint 5: Columbus's voyages should be celebrated 28
Viewpoint 6: Columbus's voyages should be protested 30
Critical Thinking Skill 3: Recognizing Stereotypes in Art 32

For Further Reading 33
Works Consulted 34
Index 35

THE PURPOSE OF THIS BOOK

An Introduction to Opposing Viewpoints

When people disagree, it is hard to figure out who is right. You may decide one person is right just because the person is your friend or a relative. But this is not a very good reason to agree or disagree with someone. It is better if you try to understand why these people disagree. On what main points do they differ? Read or listen to each person's argument carefully. Separate the facts and opinions that each person presents. Finally, decide which argument best matches what you think. This process, examining an argument without emotion, is part of what critical thinking is all about.

This is not easy. Many things make it hard to understand and form opinions. People's values, ages, and experiences all influence the way they think. This is why learning to read and think critically is an invaluable skill. Opposing Viewpoints Juniors books will help you learn and practice skills to improve your ability to read critically. By reading opposing views on an issue, you will become familiar with methods people use to attempt to convince you that their point of view is right. And you will learn to separate the authors' opinions from the facts they present.

Each Opposing Viewpoints Juniors book focuses on one critical thinking skill that will help you judge the views presented. Some of these skills are telling the difference between fact and opinion, recognizing propaganda techniques, and locating and analyzing the main idea. These skills will allow you to examine opposing viewpoints more easily.

SKILL INTRODUCTION

Recognizing Stereotypes

In this Opposing Viewpoints Juniors book, you will be asked to identify and study stereotypes. Stereotypes are exaggerated descriptions of people or things. People who use stereotypes apply a general description to a whole group. They do not look at the individual characteristics of each member of the group. Stereotyping can be favorable. For example, saying that blacks are natural basketball players is using a stereotype, but a positive one. However, most stereotyping is negative. It is meant to make fun of or belittle a person or group.

Stereotyping grows out of prejudices, beliefs, or attitudes we have about particular groups of people or things. When we stereotype people, we prejudge them. We assume that all people in a group have the same traits. For example, Mr. X thinks that all immigrants receive a "free ride" from the government. The Kaos, a family of Hmongs from Southeast Asia, happen to be his next-door neighbors. One Sunday afternoon, Mr. X notices that Mr. Kao has driven into his driveway in a brand new Toyota. While Mr. Kao's family admires the new car, Mr. X says to himself, "if it weren't for all that money they get from the government, they'd never be able to afford that new car." The idea that Mr. Kao's entire family may have pitched in or that Mr. Kao may have taken out a bank loan to buy the car never enters Mr. X's mind. Why not? Because he has prejudged all immigrants and will keep his stereotype even if it is not true.

Stereotypes are often hard to recognize because they are fixed beliefs. People have held them for a long time. While many stereotypes are easy to identify—for instance, poor people are lazy—others may be less obvious. Learning to identify stereotypes can help you tell the difference between writers who use stereotypes to further their arguments and those who do not.

You can learn to identify stereotypes by asking yourself questions about a particular reading. If a writer is talking about a group of people or a thing that he or she dislikes, these questions may help you discover stereotypes: "What is being said about this group of people or this thing? Is this group or thing being labeled unfairly?"

We asked two students to give their opinion of Christopher Columbus. Look for stereotypes in their arguments.

SAMPLE VIEWPOINT A *Maria:*

Christopher Columbus was a hero.

Christopher Columbus was the first person from Europe to bring back the knowledge of the New World. Because of Columbus, people all over Europe learned more about the world. He was a hero. He was one of the bravest men who ever lived.

I know that Columbus and his men did some bad things. But Columbus can't be blamed for that. People of his time didn't know any better. His men were Spanish, and everyone knows the Spanish are hot-tempered. They were just too hard to control. Columbus was Italian. Italians are the greatest artists, inventors, and explorers in the world. People should recognize Columbus as another great Italian. If it weren't for him, none of us would live in the United States now.

SAMPLE VIEWPOINT B *Quentin:*

Christopher Columbus was a creep.

Christopher Columbus was a total creep. I can't believe people think we should celebrate Columbus Day! Why celebrate the murder of millions of Indians? That's like celebrating the Holocaust.

Christopher Columbus made a big mistake when he got his crew from Spain. The Spanish are the most violent people on earth! In my school, we have lots of gangs, and most of the people in them are Spanish. Everyone knows that gangs are violent. When Christopher Columbus brought the Spanish to the New World, it was like letting pit bulls attack little kids. The Indians, who never did anything wrong, were just sitting around living in perfect harmony with nature. Then these horrible Spaniards started killing them.

If you ask me, we should get rid of Columbus Day and celebrate a Native American Day. On that day we could all dress up like real Indians, with tomahawks and headdresses and everything.

ANALYZING THE SAMPLE VIEWPOINTS

Maria and Quentin have very different opinions about Christopher Columbus. Both of them use stereotypes in their arguments.

Maria:

STEREOTYPES

The Spanish are hot-tempered.

Italians are the greatest artists, inventors, and explorers.

Quentin:

STEREOTYPES

The Spanish are the most violent people on earth.

Gangs are violent.

All Indians live in perfect harmony with nature.

Real Indians have tomahawks and headdresses.

In this sample, Maria and Quentin have a lot of stereotypical attitudes toward certain ethnic groups. Can you think of other examples of stereotypes you have come across in your reading or that you have heard people use?

Both Maria and Quentin think they are right about Christopher Columbus. What conclusions about Christopher Columbus could you come to from these samples? Why?

As you continue to read through the viewpoints in this book, watch for examples of stereotyping. Remember to question whether an author is portraying a group unfairly.

10   JUNIORS

CHAPTER 1

PREFACE: Did Christopher Columbus Discover the New World?

Until very recently, every schoolchild was taught that Christopher Columbus discovered the New World. Columbus was depicted as a brave and determined sailor who singlehandedly convinced Queen Isabella of Spain to fund his voyage. In history books, Columbus was portrayed as a true hero—a man who made it possible for millions of European immigrants to start fresh in a new land.

Now this image of Christopher Columbus is being challenged. Many historians and others claim that Columbus did not "discover" anything. Before he arrived, the New World already had been discovered by others—Leif Ericksson among them. In addition, the New World was already populated by over five hundred Native American tribes. To call Columbus's voyage a "discovery" would be like taking a hundred people, landing in Italy, and saying that these people discovered Italy, critics argue. Christopher Columbus may have "encountered" or "collided with" the New World, but he did not "discover" it.

Many historians argue that whether Columbus's voyages are called a discovery, an encounter, or a collision does not matter. No one can deny that Columbus made Europe aware of the New World, and that this awareness had a great impact. It was Columbus who started this new awareness. It is Columbus who should be credited with it. To celebrate Columbus's voyages is to celebrate the beginning of the world as we know it today.

The next two viewpoints debate whether Columbus should be credited with discovering the New World. Both viewpoints present stereotypes to support their case. While reading, use the margin questions to help you identify the stereotypes.

VIEWPOINT 1

Christopher Columbus should be credited with discovering the New World

Editor's Note: In the following viewpoint, the author argues that since Columbus's voyages initiated European awareness and exploration of the New World, Columbus should be credited with its discovery.

Notice how the author describes feminists, Indians, and blacks. She is stereotyping these groups.

Christopher Columbus has been attacked as a murderer and a liar. He has been blamed for all that is wrong with the treatment of Native Americans and blacks. Radical, man-hating feminists, whiny Indians, and poor blacks have all jumped on the bandwagon of Columbus haters. Does he deserve this? I say no.

Christopher Columbus was a wonderful example of a brave, determined man. He sought to bring glory and gold back to the Spanish, and, yes, a bit of fame for himself, but he also had the courage to make the voyages. Just because he thought he had landed in India, and not America, does not mean we should take credit for the discovery away from him.

12 JUNIORS

After all, what was the New World before Columbus discovered it? It was a wild, untamed land filled with uneducated and uncivilized Indians. They were so primitive, they did not even wear clothes. Columbus brought civilization to these Indians. He tried to teach them about God, and he tried to make them less barbaric.

People like to think Indians were nice all the time, but they were not. The Incas used human sacrifices in their religion. Other Indians ate human flesh. Individual life meant nothing to Indians. Indians were not individuals; they thought of themselves as part of a tribe. They did whatever the tribe wanted, even if it was murderous.

Europeans, on the other hand, had respect for individual life. Columbus and the Spaniards showed the Indians that each individual was responsible for his or her own actions.

The world we live in now would not be what it is today without the valiant efforts of Columbus and his men. Yes, there was some brutality, but that is human nature. All men instinctively want to conquer and destroy. Besides, most of the Indians died of disease, not from Columbus and his men killing them. You cannot blame Columbus for spreading germs. Remember that many other positive things happened, as well. Because of Columbus, we eat tomatoes and potatoes, we respect human rights, and millions of immigrants are free to start their lives over in this wonderful country.

> **What is the author's view of Indians? Notice how she uses negative terms to generalize about an entire group.**

> **By arguing that all men are violent, the author is stereotyping.**

How much did Columbus contribute to history?

The author argues that Columbus made many contributions to history. Name some of them. How important do you believe these contributions are? Do you, like the author, think these contributions make Columbus an important historical figure? Why or why not?

VIEWPOINT 2

Christopher Columbus did not discover the New World

Editor's Note: The author argues that Columbus does not deserve the credit for discovering the New World. She believes Columbus is an evil and mean-spirited man who deserves to be condemned, not admired.

How does the author depict the Spanish and the Indians? Are these stereotypes? How can you tell?

Christopher Columbus's discovery of the New World was not a discovery. It was a conquest. The whole idea of treating it like a discovery results in a lot of wrong ideas. For example, if Columbus "discovered" the New World, what does that say about the people who already lived there? It ignores them. It allows Europeans and Americans to think that they can just take over any land and kill whoever is on it in the name of "exploration" and "discovery." Columbus's voyages should not be admired as great accomplishments since they resulted in the bloodthirsty Spanish ruthlessly murdering thousands of peaceful, noble Native Americans. Even people who use words such as "encounter," rather than "discovery," are trying to cover up for the horrible and brutal things the Spanish did. The appropriate words for the whole mess of 1492 are "destruction," "murder," and "conquest."

"IT'S THE END OF WESTERN CIVILIZATION AS WE KNOW IT."

© Simpson/Rothco. Reprinted with permission.

14   JUNIORS

One look at the history of this time proves this is true. Bartolomé de Las Casas, who arrived in Hispaniola in 1502 and later became a priest, was an eyewitness to the murder of three thousand people:

> Such inhumanities and barbarisms were created in my sight, as no age can parallel. . . . The Spanish cut off the legs of children who ran from them. The poured people full of boiling soap. They made bets as to who, with one sweep of his sword, could cut a person in half. They loosed dogs that devoured an Indian like a hog, at first sight, in less than a moment.

The other thing wrong with calling Columbus's conquest a "discovery" is it suggests that Columbus wanted to "explore," that he wanted to participate in the noble and praiseworthy act of finding new lands. He wanted no such thing. The man was greedy and murderous. If he had wanted to explore, he would have been willing to learn from the native cultures. Instead, he took advantage of the natives' kind and gentle ways. He even tried to enslave them. As Native American author Michel Dorris says, "This harmful road into the 'New World' quickly became a ruthless, angry search for wealth."

How does the author depict Columbus's motives for his voyage? Is the author presenting an objective case? How can you tell?

Some people, most of whom are racist and pathetic Indian haters, say we should praise Columbus as a great navigator. This is laughable. The man believed he had discovered India, after all! Anyone familiar with Marco Polo's description of the Far East would have known that the New World was not India. Columbus was not only a bad navigator, but an idiot as well.

What does the author think of people who praise Columbus?

No, our nation should not celebrate Columbus's voyage as a discovery. Instead, everyone who knows the truth should join every Native American in this country to erase the name of Christopher Columbus from the history books.

What does the author believe all Native Americans think of Columbus? Is she stereotyping?

Should Columbus be condemned?

In this viewpoint, the author dismisses Columbus as a stupid, brutal man. Do you think Columbus should be viewed in this way? Why or why not?

CRITICAL THINKING SKILL 1
Recognizing Stereotypes

After reading the two viewpoints on whether Columbus should be honored as the discoverer of the New World, make a chart similar to the one made for Maria and Quentin on page 10. List the stereotypes each author uses to make her case. Remember that many of the stereotypes in these readings have already been pointed out to you. Take a few minutes to review the questions in the margins of the readings before making your list. A chart is started for you below:

Viewpoint 1:
STEREOTYPES

Radical, man-hating feminists, whiny Indians, and poor blacks have all jumped on the bandwagon of Columbus haters.

Viewpoint 2:
STEREOTYPES

Bloodthirsty Spanish.

Noble Indians.

Which viewpoint contains the most stereotypes? After reading the two viewpoints, which did you think was the most convincing? Why? List some stereotypes that you have heard about Indians and Hispanics that have not been mentioned in the viewpoints.

CHAPTER 2

PREFACE: Is Christopher Columbus's Legacy in the New World Positive?

The legacy of Christopher Columbus is very controversial. For many, it is nothing more than cruelty, brutality, and death. As author Barry Lopez states:

> We lost whole communities of people, plants, and animals because a handful of men wanted gold and silver, title to land, the privileges of aristocracy, slaves, stables of little boys. We lost languages, . . . books, ceremonies, systems of logic and metaphysics—a long, hideous carnage.

These are the incidents that Lopez and others want educators and the public to remember about Columbus. They want people to think of Columbus as a symbol of all that is wrong with European and American history: intolerance, slavery, racism, the stealing and taking over of land, and the destruction of native ways. In this context, Columbus is a medieval Hitler, or worse. Russell Means, a Native American activist, claims that Columbus "makes Hitler look like a juvenile delinquent."

On the opposing side are people who believe that Columbus, while not perfect, brought European values, such as respect for individual rights, to the New World. These values remain of lasting importance to everyone.

Writer and *New Republic* editor Charles Krauthammer acknowledges that Columbus committed some crimes against Native Americans. But, he claims,

> What eventually grew on this bloodied soil? The answer is the great modern civilization of the Americas—a new world of individual rights, an ever expanding circle of liberty, and twice in this century a savior of the world from totalitarian barbarism.

Krauthammer and others believe that if we blame Columbus for his mistakes, we must also credit him for the positive parts of his legacy—bringing European civilization and ideas to the New World.

In the following viewpoints, Columbus's legacy is discussed. Try to identify stereotypes in the arguments.

CHRISTOPHER COLUMBUS **17**

VIEWPOINT 3

Christopher Columbus's legacy is negative

Editor's Note: In the following viewpoint, the author recounts all the things she believes Columbus wrought in the New World and declares that Columbus did nothing positive. As you read, attempt to recognize and identify stereotypes the author uses.

Do you think the author's depiction of the history of the world is accurate? Why or why not?

The history of the New World since the time of Columbus has been one of continual murder, colonialism, and enslavement of native peoples. This whole legacy began with Christopher Columbus and his destruction of the lands he is credited with "discovering."

Columbus left his mark on history, all right. But that mark is a deep, open wound. Because of Columbus, European monarchs thought they could enslave and murder people. They thought they could grab any land they could get their hands on. Because of Columbus, native peoples were, and still are, considered less than human.

On October 4, 1492, two days after his landing in the New World, Columbus wrote to the queen and king of Spain about his plans to exploit the peoples of the New World:

How does Columbus stereotype the Indians in his letter?

> Your Highness may, whenever you so wish, have all sent to Castille or keep them all captives in the island, for with fifty armed men you will keep them all under your sway and will make them do all you may desire.

To induce the natives to bring him gold, Columbus established a quota for each person. If the native did not make the quota, his or her hands or feet were chopped off.

18   JUNIORS

Bartolemé de Las Casas reported in his History of the Indies *that the Spaniards would set their dogs upon the natives.*

This is the legacy that has been handed down from Columbus. People are chess pieces to be moved around by those who are more powerful. If people are nice, they can be used and manipulated.

Alex Ewen is the editor of the journal *Native Nations* and a member of the Purepecha Indian nation of northern Mexico. He says Columbus

> was possessed by an ethic of destruction. The idea that people could be property, that the earth could be a property, was an idea alien to Indians. [Native Americans] see him sort of like a creature out of science fiction, an alien from another planet who sort of zipped down and imposed a new way of life, against which there has been a guerrilla struggle to this day.

The world Columbus entered, and that we lost, was perfect. It was as close to the Garden of Eden as humans are likely to get. Kirkpatrick Sale describes this blissful state in his book, *The Conquest of Paradise*. He portrays the Tainos, the Indians Columbus met:

> The Taino had developed a social system that had refined the arts of civility and harmony to a degree that was remarkable. So little a role did violence play in their life that they seemed to have had a society without war and essentially even without individual violence. Columbus described them as: 'In all the world there is no better people nor better country. They love their neighbors as themselves and they have the sweetest talk in the world and are gentle and are always laughing.

How do the author and Kirkpatrick Sale categorize the world before Columbus? Are they stereotyping? How can you tell?

CHRISTOPHER COLUMBUS **19**

PLAGUES AND DISEASE

The diseases which invading powers brought with them to the Americas continue to devastate peoples who inhabit the remotest regions of this continent.

- Fifteen major epidemics raged through the Americas within a century of Columbus: 40 to 50 million Native Americans died by the year 1600, equivalent to half a billion people today.
- Old World pathogens swept the land, killing between a third and a half of the people in the Inca empire. From 1635-40 nearly half the Huron people in 'New France' died from diseases brought by Jesuit missionaries and traders.
- Today isolated native groups still die from common diseases to which they have no immunities. When miners invaded their land in the late 1980s nearly 2,000 Yanomami Indians in northern Brazil died in the first two years. Survival International says the Yanomami may disappear within a decade.

Sources: *Columbus: His Enterprise—Exploding the Myth*, Hans Konig (Monthly Review Press/Latin America Bureau, 1991). 'The Jesuits and the Fur Trade,' Bruce Trigger, from *Sweet Promises*, ed. J R Miller, (U of T Press, Toronto, 1991). Yanomami Survival Campaign, Survival International, London, UK, 1990. Photo: Bettmann.

A group of Yanomami Indians in Brazil protest the destruction of their rainforest environment by gold miners.

How does the author depict businesspeople? Is this depiction fair, or is it a stereotype?

Is this an overly complimentary picture of Indian society, or does it seem accurate? How can you tell?

Look at the world now. Those gentle, noble souls are gone. The world is populated with ruthless businesspeople who care nothing about the common person. Forests are destroyed by heartless loggers who simply want to make a quick buck off our natural wonders. And the nation's Indians live in filthy squalor, dying of alcoholism and disease, because the federal government does not care about these nonwhites.

Indian societies were far superior to European societies of Columbus's time. In the fifteenth century, European monarchs were competing to see who could kill more people. Medicine in medieval Europe was a joke. In contrast, writer Michael Aaron Rockland points out, Indian societies were

> doing brain surgery and had elaborate astronomical observatories at a time when such things did not exist in Europe and people who tried to widen Europeans' scientific knowledge were burned at the stake.

The spread of European culture and the loss of Indian culture has left modern society without a soul. Americans today are senseless and uncaring about the environment, other living things, and each other. How do we return to the paradise of the past? Can we start over? In *The Conquest of Paradise*, Sale quotes an Irokwa woman from New York City who has the answer:

> Now [the whites] come to gather for the coming disaster and destruction of the white man *by his own hands*, with his own progressive, advanced, technological devices, that only the American Indian can avert. Now the time is near. And it is only the Indian who knows the cure. It is only the Indian who can stop this plague.

Greed, racism, and the rape of the land are the legacy of Columbus. He was the first. His encounter set the stage. To change this, we must try to find the path back to the noble savage—those gentle Tainos. Only in the peaceful and lovely ways of the Indians can humanity find its salvation.

Eric Joselyn. Reprinted with permission.

> **Is Columbus to blame?**
>
> The author blames many wrongs in the world on Christopher Columbus. Do you think Columbus can be held responsible for all of these things? Why or why not? What was Columbus's original purpose in coming to the New World?

VIEWPOINT 4 Christopher Columbus's legacy is positive

Editor's Note: In this viewpoint, the author argues that Columbus's voyages and subsequent impact on history were positive. She sees many good things that came out of the meeting between Columbus and the New World. As you read, look for stereotypes. How do this viewpoint's stereotypes differ from those in Viewpoint 3?

From the first paragraph of this viewpoint, you can detect the author's opinion. Watch for stereotypes the author may use to defend her position.

With the uproar made by Native Americans and other Indian sympathizers over the brutality of Columbus, everyone seems to be forgetting a good deal of historical fact. Columbus was not perfect—who is? But we should not forget that he accomplished "possibly the most important thing that had happened to the world since the birth of Christ," as Frank Donatelli, chairman of the Christopher Columbus Quincentenary Jubilee Commission, says.

What was that important thing? It was the bringing of Western civilization to a bunch of scattered tribes that could not even communicate with one another because they had no common language. Indian lovers and apologists are always carping about how many different Indian tribes there were as though this was some kind of great accomplishment. There were so many tribes because they could not learn from one another. And many of these tribes could hardly be called civilizations.

THE COLUMBIAN EXCHANGE

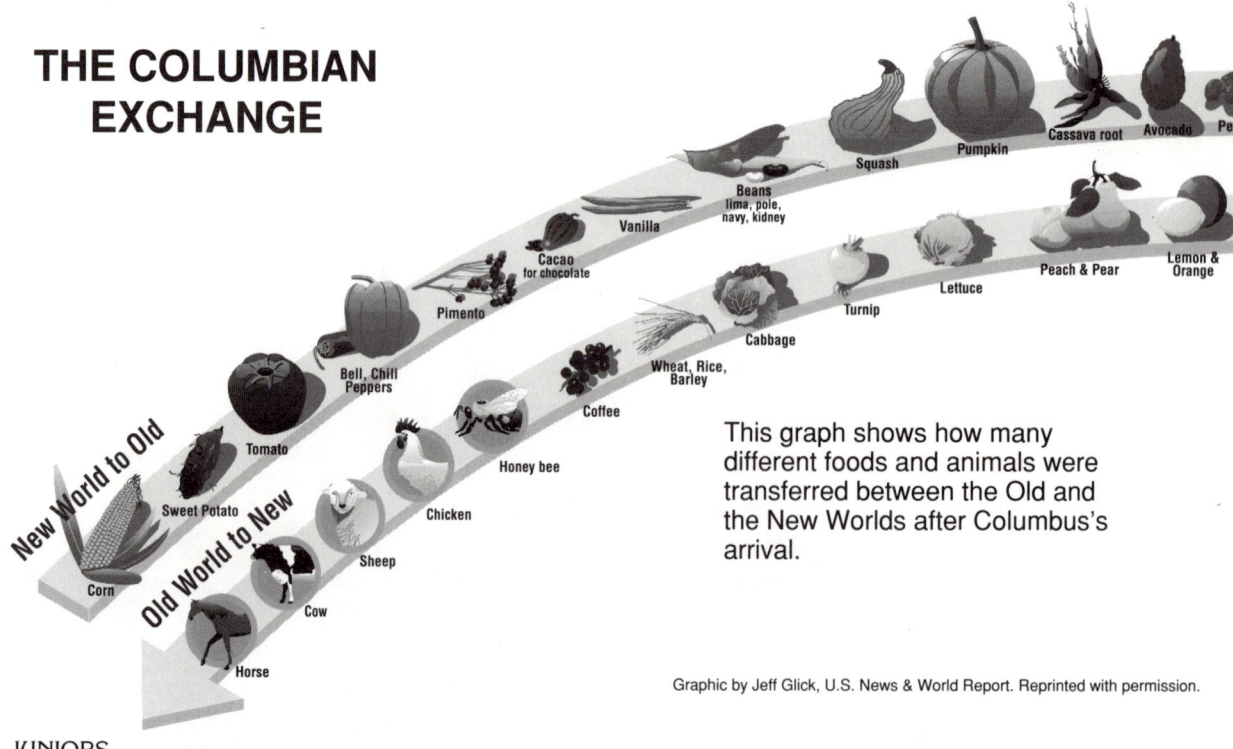

This graph shows how many different foods and animals were transferred between the Old and the New Worlds after Columbus's arrival.

Graphic by Jeff Glick, U.S. News & World Report. Reprinted with permission.

Criticisms of Columbus are born of ignorance. Why were these great Indian societies so easy to conquer, for example? Most of them, like the Incas, had ridiculous bureaucracies. When Pizarro, a Spanish explorer after Columbus, conquered the Incas, all he had to do was nab the monarch called the "Inca," and the whole society crumbled. Not one person could do anything to save the society because no one knew what to do. They were all mindless slaves who did not know how to think for themselves.

In contrast, Western society gave birth to individual thought and responsibility. Columbus brought these ideas to the New World. Do we want to return to a world where we all slavishly follow a ruler, whether he is right or wrong? Of course not! Then let's stop romanticizing these primitive, inefficient Indians.

One of the people who is often quoted in the attacks on Columbus is Bartolomé de Las Casas. He was the adventurer-turned-priest who condemned Columbus's treatment of the Indians. In fact, many people in Europe protested this treatment. But this just proves again how superior the Europeans were. Native Americans would not have dared to challenge the great Inca or the great Aztec leader over their poor treatment.

Native American societies did not revere individual life. Inca and Aztec leaders used their people like slaves, just as the ancient Egyptians did. It took Europeans to bring ideas of individual worth to the New World. As Robert Royal, resident scholar at the American Enterprise Institute, points out, native peoples were not

The author uses the Incas to generalize about all Indians. Is this fair, or is it an example of stereotyping? Why?

What adjectives does the author use to describe Indians? Why is this an example of stereotyping?

CHRISTOPHER COLUMBUS **23**

In this stylized illustration of Columbus's landing, Columbus and his men thank Christ for bringing them safely to the New World as the natives look on.

by and large, respectful of other Indian peoples, whom they considered as alien as the white man. From what we know about these societies—and we know quite a lot—ideas like minority rights and pluralism played no role in their political organization.

People like author Kirkpatrick Sale would like us to believe that *all* Indians were peaceful and loving and all Europeans were bad. That is nothing but a stereotype. As author Cathy Booth says, Sale makes Indians look like "a bunch of New Agers vacationing in the Bahamas." Sale forgets to mention that the Tainos had a social structure with wealthy people at the top and slaves at the bottom.

Europeans did not invent slavery and cruelty. Indians were plenty cruel. For example, the Aztecs, in their wonderful culture, believed that they had to sacrifice humans in order to keep demons from leaping from the sky. Should we return to this society?

The Indians did not live in perfect harmony with the environment, either. There is a lot of evidence that many of these cultures had to move to new locations because their populations grew and they used up the resources. But do we say Indians "raped the land"? No. But they did.

Finally, tally up the accomplishments of the Europeans, the Americans, and the Indians. It seems to me that all we lost is some pretty beadwork and a few nice legends. On the side of Western society, we have the Renaissance. We have people of great accomplishments like Michelangelo, Raphael, da Vinci, Erasmus,

In contrast to much of this viewpoint, the author is not using stereotypes in this paragraph. She is actually contradicting a common stereotype. What is it?

Thomas More, Martin Luther, and Thomas Jefferson. It seems obvious to me that Europeans are the ones that have the better society.

All of us, as author Robert Royal claims,

> owe a debt of gratitude to the man who, in spite of many faults, began the intermixing of the Old and the New World, and who, wittingly or unwittingly, started us all toward an entirely new vision of our common human life on earth.

Jean-Baptiste Charcot, another explorer, charted much of Antarctica's coastline early in this century. He comes to a similar conclusion about Columbus. He writes, "His ships have sailed into history. The achievement of Christopher Columbus is so impressive that it moves us to the point of great rapture."

Think about it.

> **What does the author say we lost from the Indians? What does she say we gained from Europe? Are either of these descriptions stereotypical? Why or why not?**

MANY STATES ARE NAMED AFTER INDIAN TRIBES

Indiana is one of the more aptly named states. Settlers wanted to show that it had been "the land of the Indians." The names of 26 of the 49 other states are derived from Indian words.

Alabama. Choctaw for "clearers of the thicket"
Alaska. Aleut for "great land"
Arizona. Papago for "place of little springs"
Arkansas. Sioux for a small tribe known as "the people who live downstream"
Connecticut. Pequot for "at the long tidal river"
Idaho. Shoshone for "the sun is coming up"
Illinois. For "superior men," what the Illinois Indians called themselves
Iowa. Sioux for "sleepy ones"
Kansas. Kansa for "people of the south wind"
Kentucky. Cherokee for "meadowland"
Massachusetts. Algonquian for "people near the great hill," a spot outside Boston
Michigan. Algonquian for "big lake"
Minnesota. Sioux for "sky-tinted water"
Mississippi. Ojibwa for "big river"
Missouri. Sioux for a tribe known as "people with the dugout canoes"
Nebraska. Oto for "flat water"
New Mexico. From the Aztec "Mexica," followers of the war god Mexitli
North Dakota, South Dakota. Sioux for "friends"
Ohio. Wyandot for "beautiful river"
Oklahoma. Choctaw for "red people"
Tennessee. Cherokee for "area of traveling waters"
Texas. Caddo for "ally," a word for the Tejas Indians
Utah. Ute for "land of the sun"
Wisconsin. Chippewa for "gathering of the waters"
Wyoming. Algonquian for "upon the great plain"

> **Columbus's contributions**
>
> What is the author's opinion of Christopher Columbus's contributions to the New World? How does it differ from the opinion of the opposing viewpoint? After reading these two viewpoints, do you think Columbus's legacy is positive, negative, or a little of both? Explain your answer.

CHRISTOPHER COLUMBUS

CRITICAL THINKING SKILL 2

Recognizing Stereotypes in Statements

Below is a list of statements related to Christopher Columbus. Consider each statement carefully. Mark S for any statement that is an example of stereotyping. Mark N for any statement that is not a stereotype. Mark U if you are undecided about any statement. Then give a brief explanation of why you decided on your answer.

EXAMPLE: Before Christopher Columbus, the New World was a peaceful place without war, cruelty, or violence.

ANSWER: S. Stereotype. Some native cultures were peaceful, but others were violent, and many native tribes warred against one another.

1. After a voyage of more than two years and many difficulties, Christopher Columbus reached the New World. What he found was a world of endless variety—new plants, new peoples, and new civilizations.

    Answer _____ Explanation _____
    _____

2. Europeans were far superior to the native cultures of the New World. The Europeans wore clothes, had an organized religion, and had created many wonderful works of art.

    Answer _____ Explanation _____
    _____

3. The Incas were a bloodthirsty, brutal lot.

    Answer _____ Explanation _____
    _____

4. People who wish to praise Columbus's accomplishments are nothing but a group of racists who would like nothing more than to kill off the rest of the Native Americans living in the United States.

    Answer _____ Explanation _____
    _____

5. Columbus's legacy is alive and well today in American businesses. America's businesspeople care nothing about people, land, or culture. All they want to do is make money.

    Answer _____ Explanation _____
    _____

6. One of the consequences of the encounter between the Old and New Worlds was that many thousands of Indians died from Old World diseases such as smallpox.

    Answer _____ Explanation _____
    _____

CHAPTER 3

PREFACE: Should Columbus's Voyages Be Celebrated?

In 1992, a battle was fought over how the Quincentenary of Columbus's voyage should be observed. All over the world, people lined up on one side or another: Should Columbus's 500th anniversary be celebrated, or protested?

As the world becomes more sensitive to the treatment and history of native peoples, many people believe it is wrong to continue to honor Columbus. Such celebrations ignore the fact that thousands of native people were tortured, killed, and relocated to make way for the Europeans. It is an important issue today, many believe, because natives in countries such as Brazil, Belize, and El Salvador continue to be discriminated against, threatened, and driven from their mountain and forest homes. Forget about Columbus Day, many argue, or remember it as a day of infamy.

Many Native Americans feel especially offended by the holiday. Suzan Shown Harjo, who is Cheyenne and Creek, is president and director of the Morning Star Foundation, a group organized to protest the celebration of Columbus's voyage. Harjo argues:

> As Native American peoples in this red quarter of Mother Earth, we have no reason to celebrate an invasion that caused the demise of so many of our people and is still causing destruction today. The Europeans stole our land and killed our people.

Many people of diverse backgrounds have formed a group on the opposing side of the debate. They view the Quincentenary as a celebration of the joining of the New and Old Worlds, as well as an opportunity to reeducate people about the full meaning of the encounter—the good along with the bad. James Muldoon, professor of history at Rutgers University in Camden, New Jersey, is one person who holds this view. He writes:

> Should we, then, celebrate Columbus? Certainly. He was a brave man whose actions made a major contribution to the formation of the modern world. Should we celebrate equally each and every consequence of Columbus's first voyage? Of course not, but then neither did many of his contemporaries. We praise the good and condemn the bad. To reject Columbus is in effect to reject the modern world.

Many Native Americans, too, see the celebration of Columbus's voyage as an opportunity. Rather than abstaining from the celebration, many wish to commemorate it with events that focus attention on native peoples and their problems.

The following viewpoints present different approaches to commemorating Columbus. Look for stereotypes in the authors' arguments.

VIEWPOINT 5 Columbus's voyages should be celebrated

Editor's Note: In the following viewpoint, the author argues that Columbus Day must continue to be celebrated. In it, she shows a distinct bias that leads her to use stereotypes. Use the questions in the margins to guide you in identifying these stereotypes.

What "we" is the author referring to? Who does the "we" leave out? How do you think this assumption might bias her discussion of Columbus and Native Americans?

How does the author depict men? Is this a stereotype? Why or why not?

"If you put down Columbus, you put down the entire Renaissance," says Anne Paolucci, president of Columbus: Countdown 1992. This statement makes it clear why we should continue to celebrate Columbus's voyages. They were part of a mass enlightenment—a time of discovery, invention, and artistic achievement that remains unparalleled today. No other civilization or time period compares. And one of the crowning glories of this amazing time period was Columbus's discovery of the New World.

I grant that Columbus may have been a bad governor who let brutal things happen to the Indians, but this should not take away from Columbus's real achievements. Men will be men, after all. Give them a new continent to conquer, and the thirst for power will take over.

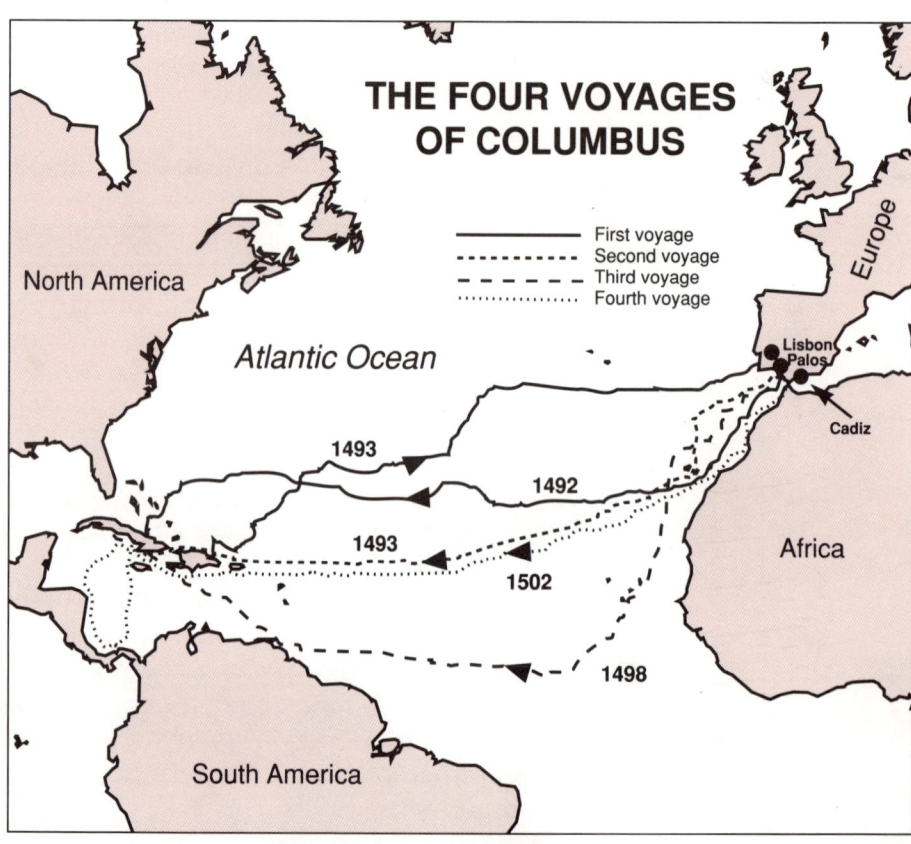

28 JUNIORS

But celebrating Columbus is not about arguing the good and the bad. As author Jon Margolis states, "Arguing about whether the European conquest of America was 'a good thing' is a fool's errand. It was an inevitable thing, its cruelties and its glories both."

When we celebrate Columbus's achievements, we are celebrating our civilization. And we have a lot to celebrate. For example, after Columbus's discovery, Pizarro destroyed Incan civilization, which many ignorant people want us to mourn. But I would not want to live like the Incas. Their society was brutal, dictatorial, and inefficient. By contrast, our society, the one Columbus brought from Europe, is a wonderful example of liberty and individualism. As Charles Krauthammer writes:

> Is it Eurocentric to believe the life of liberty is superior? . . . After 500 years the Columbian legacy has created a civilization that we ought not, in all humble piety . . . , declare to be no better or worse than that of the Incas. It turned out better. And mankind is the better for it. Definitely better. Reason enough to honor Columbus and bless 1492.

How does the author depict European society? What information do you know that contradicts this stereotype?

Columbus represents a lot of things that are right with the New World. The spirit of adventurism and discovery that drove Columbus is the selfsame spirit that drove the rugged pioneers to settle the untamed wilderness of North America. This spirit also inspired Columbus to try many unusual foods from the New World and take back what have become the staples of Europe—potatoes and corn. Raymond Sokolov, author of *Why We Eat What We Eat: How the Encounter Between the New World and the Old Changed the Way Everyone on the Planet Eats*, writes:

> Human life is more varied and interesting everywhere today because of the exchange of foods and food ideas that Columbus made possible. Few people eat a diet similar to what they would have eaten 500 years ago. . . . Raise a glass of Coke—and wish yourself happy 500th. Let's hear it for Columbus.

Does the author stereotype America's pioneers? How can you tell?

Let us continue to honor and commemorate Columbus for his bravery and ingenuity, and for the birth of our civilization. To do less would be to lie to ourselves—and our children—about the superiority of our modern world.

What should we commemorate on Columbus Day?

Name three of the things the author says we should thank Columbus for. Do you agree with the author on why we should celebrate Columbus Day? Why or why not?

VIEWPOINT 6 Columbus's voyages should be protested

Editor's Note: The author uses many quotes in her viewpoint to support her argument that Columbus Day should not be celebrated. Note the qualifications of the people the author quotes. What bias might these people have? How might that influence their arguments?

Native American Suzan Shown Harjo is president and director of the Morning Star Foundation, a group organized to protest the celebration of Columbus. She gives an eloquent summation of why Columbus Day should be relegated to the dustbin of history. Harjo writes that European and American societies

> must come to grips with the past, acknowledge responsibility for the present, and do something about the future. It does no good to gloss over the history of excesses of Western civilization, especially when those excesses are the root cause of deplorable conditions today.

To celebrate Columbus is to ignore history. It is to say that Native Americans no longer exist, just as Columbus and other whites who followed in his spirit of murder wanted. But Native Americans have not disappeared. And they remember well what Columbus did. As Hans Konig, author of *Columbus: His Enterprise: Exploding the Myth,* writes:

Columbus's men use their superior weapons to defeat Native Americans.

30 JUNIORS

Columbus had promised mountains of gold to his backers and his effort to squeeze this wealth out of the simple native society of the island [Hispaniola, where Columbus first landed] caused the death of half Its population between 1492 and 1500. . . . Within two generations the entire nation was wiped out. . . . In those eight years there is not one recorded moment of awe, of joy, of love, of a smile. There is only anger, cruelty, gold, terror, and death. We either use [the Quincentenary] to rethink our history, or we ignore the record and we celebrate.

Instead of celebration, we should use this time for protest. We should join Native Americans, who continue to struggle for justice. We should recognize that these people are not invisible. They all continue to struggle against white oppression. We should join them in their struggle against white ruination, disrespect for the earth, and against the white scourge—alcohol—that has been used against Indians for over five hundred years.

For too long, Columbus has basked in the glory of honor and worship. North Americans must topple him off his pedestal. In his place, let us honor the Native American.

How does Konig depict early civilizations? Do you think this an overly positive stereotype? Why?

What has white civilization done to the Indians, according to the author? Are any of these examples stereotypes of Indians or of whites?

Does celebrating Columbus Day dishonor Native Americans?

The author of this viewpoint feels strongly that celebrating Columbus betrays the history of Native Americans. Do you agree? Why or why not? How much were you told in school about Columbus's impact on Native Americans? If you were told little about his impact, how does that affect your answer?

CHRISTOPHER COLUMBUS **31**

CRITICAL THINKING SKILL 3

Recognizing Stereotypes in Art

In this activity, you will be asked to look at several pictures. Just as writers can be guilty of stereotyping to persuade the reader of their viewpoint, artists can also use stereotypes. The pictures below all contain stereotypes of Native Americans, Europeans, or Christopher Columbus. After looking at these pictures, ask yourself the questions listed below. If you are doing this activity as part of a larger group or class, compare your answers with others. In this way, you may become aware of further stereotyping.

Questions:

1. What point of view does the artist embrace, that of Europeans or that of Native Americans?
2. How are the different groups of people portrayed in each picture?
3. Are any of these portrayals stereotypes? Are any of them overly negative or positive? Identify each stereotype that you see in the pictures. Explain your choices.
4. What do you think the artist's purpose is in each of these drawings? How can you tell?

Columbus's first landing.

This Aztec drawing depicts the cruelty of the Spaniards.

This horrific scene was originally an illustration to accompany de Las Casas' text. The men and women who are strung up are Native Americans.

An illustration depicts the Native Americans viciously slaughtering white settlers.

32 JUNIORS

FOR FURTHER READING

The author recommends the following books and periodicals for further research on the topic. Check the works consulted list that follows for further suggestions.

Ricardo Caballero Aquino, "Looking Back—Latin America's Burden," *The Christian Science Monitor*, February 12, 1992.

Christopher Columbus, *The Log of Christopher Columbus*. Translated by Robert H. Suson. Camden, ME: International Marine Publishing, 1987.

Michael Dorris, "Native Savages? We'll Drink to That," *The New York Times*, April 21, 1992.

Martin Espada, "Putting Columbus in His Place: Two Worlds Didn't Collide in 1492, One Steamrolled the Other," *The Christian Science Monitor*, March 11, 1992.

Benjamin Keen, tr., *The Life of the Admiral Christopher Columbus by His Son Ferdinand*. New Brunswick, NJ: Rutgers University Press, 1959.

Bartolomé de Las Casas, *The Devastation of the Indies: A Brief Account*. Translated by Herman Briffault. New York: The Seabury Press, 1974.

Elizabeth Martinez, "A Chicana Look at 500 Years," *Z*, January 1992.

Monthly Review, "Columbus and the New World Order: 1492-1992." Special Issue, July/August 1992.

Robert Allen Warrior, "Columbus Quincentennial Is Nothing to Celebrate," *Utne Reader*, November/December 1991.

Loretta J. Williams, "Celebrate What?: Can We Use the Columbus Quincentenary to Forge a New Politics of Equality and Understanding?" *Democratic Left*, May/June 1992.

WORKS CONSULTED

The following books and periodicals were used in the compilation of this book.

Joel Achenbach, "Debating Columbus in a New World: Is This About Defining the Past or the Future?" *The Washington Post National Weekly Edition*, October 7-13, 1991. Article provides a broad overview of different pro/con arguments surrounding Columbus and his legacy. Lots of good quotes.

Bill Bigelow, et al., eds., *Rethinking Columbus*. Special issue of *Rethinking Schools*. Available from *Rethinking Schools*, 1001 E. Keefe Ave., Milwaukee, WI 53212. Excellent collection of articles, poetry, and illustrations that are critical of Columbus and his enterprise. Contains articles by Bigelow, Susan Shown Harjo, and others.

Warren H. Carroll, "The Historical Truth About Christopher Columbus," *Fidelity*, April 1992. A scholar defends Columbus and his enterprise.

Wayne Ellwood, "Hidden History Columbus and the Colonial Legacy," *New Internationalist*, December 1991. Article is accompanied by several excellent charts and graphs documenting the destruction of Native lands and peoples by colonialism, disease, slavery, and other causes.

Mark Ely, "The True Story of the Columbus Invasion," *Revolutionary Worker*, October 13, 1991. The story of Columbus from a communist perspective.

Charles Krauthammer, "Hail Columbus, Dead White Male," *Time*, May 27, 1991. Krauthammer criticizes those who attack Columbus. Supports Columbus's achievements.

James Muldoon, "The Columbus Quincentennial: Should Christians Celebrate It?" *America*, October 27, 1990. A Catholic clergyman concludes that the quincentennial should be a time to reflect on Christianity and its effects.

Newsweek, "1492-1992, When Worlds Collide: How Columbus's Voyages Transformed Both East and West." Special Issue, Fall/Winter 1991. Good collection of articles that examine Columbus from a variety of different perspectives.

Robert Royal, "Columbus as a Dead European Male: The Ideological Underpinnings of the Controversy over 1492," *The World & I*, December 1991. Excellent defense of Columbus on historical and moral grounds.

Kirpatrick Sale, *The Conquest of Paradise*. New York: Alfred A. Knopf, 1990. A contemporary environmentalist/activist writes a scathing attack on Columbus. Perhaps the most critical attack of Columbus to date.

U.S. News & World Report, "America Before Columbus." Special Issue, July 8, 1991. Good overview of Columbus the man, his voyages, and his legacy. Excellent charts and graphs.

Herman J. Viola and Carolyn Margolis, eds., *Seeds of Change: A Quincentennial Commemoration*. Washington, DC: Smithsonian Institution Press, 1991. This unique collection of essays covers many different aspects of Columbus's impact on the New World and vice versa.

INDEX

Aztecs, 23
  cruelty of, 24

Booth, Cathy, 24

Charcot, Jean-Baptiste, 25
Christopher Columbus
  Quincentenary
  Jubilee Commission, 22
colonialism, 18
Columbus, Christopher
  as bad governor, 28
  as discoverer of New World, 12-13
    con, 14-15
  as hero, 8
  as murderer, 9
  legacy of, 17
    as negative, 18-21
    as positive, 22-25
  treatment of in history, 11
  voyages should be celebrated, 28-29
  voyages should be protested, 30-31

Da Vinci, Leonardo, 24
disease
  effect on Native Americans, 20
Donatelli, Frank, 22
Dorris, Michael
  criticisms of Columbus, 15

environment
  destruction of, 20, 21

Erasmus, 24
Ericksson, Leif, 11
European culture
  as advanced, 13, 22, 24, 29
  as cruel, 14, 20-21, 30
  wrongs of, 14
Ewen, Alex, 19

feminists, 12

Harjo, Susan Shown, 27, 30

Incas, 23, 29
Isabella, Queen, 11

Jefferson, Thomas, 25

Konig, Hans, 30-31
Krauthammer, Charles, 17, 29

Las Casas, Bartolemé de, 15, 23
Lopez, Barry, 17
Luther, Martin, 25

Margolis, Jon, 29
Means, Russell, 17
Michelangelo, 24
Morning Star Foundation, 27, 30
Muldoon, James, 27

Native Americans
  as primitive, 13
  criticisms of Columbus, 30
  as unjustified, 12, 22

  con, 20-21
  culture of
    as inferior to European, 22-23
  poor treatment of, 18-19
New World
  as untamed wilderness, 13

Paolucci, Anne, 28
Pizarro, 23, 29
Polo, Marco, 15

quincentenary
  arguments over, 27

racism, 17
Raphael, 24
Renaissance, 24
Rockland, Michael Aaron, 20
Royal, Robert, 23-24, 25

Sale, Kirkpatrick, 21
  criticisms of, 24
  opinion of Native Americans, 19-20
slavery, 17, 18
Sokolov, Raymond, 29
Spaniards
  as murderers, 9, 14
states
  list of those named after tribes, 25

Tainos, 21, 24

Yanomami, 20